Monkey's Big

Story by Annette Smith
Illustrations by Chantal Stewart

Here comes Monkey.

Monkey is on a big bike.

"Look at my bike,"

 said Monkey.

"My bike is **big**."

"My bike is little,"
said Little Teddy.

Look at Little Teddy.

"Little Teddy," said Rabbit,

"Monkey's bike is too big."

Little Teddy is on the big bike!

"Oh, no!" said Rabbit.

"Little Teddy," said Monkey,

"here is the little bike."

Little Teddy is happy.

Rabbit is happy, too.